# SMIPLIFIED SEO FUNDAMENTALS FOR BEGINNERS

A step to step guide to dominate search engine ranking

## Jeff Philips

# Simplified SEO

**Fundamentals for Beginners**

*A step to step guide to dominate search engine ranking*

Jeff Philips

# DISCLAIMER

Despite making every effort to be as precise and thorough as possible, the Publisher does not at any time guarantee or suggest that the contents of this report are correct due to the Internet's tendency to change quickly.

Although every effort has been made to verify the content of this publication, the Publisher disclaims all liability for any mistakes, omissions, or other interpretations of the subject matter. Any perceived slights towards particular people, groups, or organizations are accidental.

Like everything else in life, there are no guarantees of income in books with practical advice. Readers are advised to respond based on their own judgment regarding their own circumstances and take appropriate action.

This book is not meant to be a source for accounting, financial, legal, or business advice. All readers are urged to consult with qualified experts in the fields of law, business, accounting, and finance

# Table of Contents



- Content

- Title Tag

- URL

- Meta Description

- Headlines

- User Experience



- Comparing Good and Bad Links

- Hyperlinks and Search Engines



- When Content Marketing and SEO Collide

- The Execution Procedure



- Position for Keywords

- Search Intent

- Page Speed

- Utilize HTTPS

- Prevent Duplicate Content

- Optimize Your Images

- Link Building Importance For SEO

## Introduction

Welcome to the definitive guide on Search Engine Optimization (SEO), a comprehensive resource that will empower you to navigate the dynamic landscape of digital marketing and drive your online presence to new heights. In this book, we will embark on a journey through the intricate world of SEO, exploring its key principles, strategies, and techniques that are crucial for achieving visibility, authority, and success in the digital realm.

Whether you're a seasoned marketer, a business owner, a content creator, or a curious individual seeking to demystify the complexities of SEO, this book has been meticulously crafted to provide you with the knowledge, insights, and practical steps required to excel in the ever-evolving realm of search engines. We will delve into the intricacies of keyword research, content optimization, technical SEO, link building, and more, unraveling the secrets that underpin search engine algorithms and user behavior.

As the digital landscape continues to evolve, SEO remains a cornerstone of online success. By mastering the principles outlined in this book, you'll gain the tools and strategies needed to not only adapt to the changing search landscape but also to thrive in it. Prepare to embark on a transformative journey that will equip you with the expertise to enhance your website's visibility, connect with your target audience, and achieve remarkable results in the world of SEO.

In today's interconnected world, where a vast majority of online experiences begin with a search engine query, the art and science of SEO have become more crucial than ever. This book is designed to be your compass through the intricate terrain of SEO, helping you navigate the challenges, seize the opportunities, and unlock the potential of your digital presence.

In the chapters ahead, we will not only uncover the foundational principles of SEO but also explore advanced strategies that can set you apart from the competition. We'll unravel the mysteries of on-page optimization, guiding you in crafting compelling and informative content that resonates with both users and search engines. You'll gain insights into the ever-evolving landscape of search algorithms, learning how to adapt your strategies to stay ahead in the game.

Moreover, technical SEO will no longer be a daunting enigma, as we dissect the intricacies of website architecture, speed optimization, mobile responsiveness, and more. You'll discover how to create a website that not only impresses human visitors but also communicates effectively with search engine crawlers.

Link building, often referred to as the backbone of SEO, will be demystified as well. You'll learn how to cultivate high-quality backlinks that establish your website as a reputable authority in your field, fostering not only search engine trust but also enhancing your brand's credibility.

But SEO is not solely about tactics and techniques. We'll explore the bigger picture—how SEO fits into your overall digital marketing strategy, how it aligns with your brand's identity, and how it contributes to achieving your business goals. Whether you're aiming to increase e-commerce sales, boost blog readership, or drive local foot traffic, SEO will be your ally in reaching those aspirations.

As you immerse yourself in the pages that follow, remember that SEO is an ongoing journey. The search landscape is ever-evolving, and staying up-to-date with the latest trends, algorithm changes, and user behaviors will be essential to maintaining your competitive edge. This book is not a one-time read; it's a valuable reference that you can revisit throughout your SEO odyssey.

So, whether you're a marketer seeking to optimize client websites, an entrepreneur aiming to scale your business, or a curious mind eager to comprehend the mechanics of search engines, this book is your guide. Get ready to equip yourself with the knowledge, tools, and insights that will empower you to conquer the digital realm through the art of SEO.

## Chapter One

## What is SEO

Due to the dominance of social media and online activity in our lives, it is now essential for businesses to focus on the various techniques that enhance their online presence.

They increasingly focus on hiring specialists whose sole responsibility it is to develop new strategies that aid them in growing their online traffic. Most of the time, search engines like Google direct and reroute this traffic. Search engine optimization has evolved into a crucial component of the business in order to delight them.

Now, a large portion of this traffic redirection is intended to occur naturally. You may ensure (to some extent) that your website never disappears from the search engines' radar if you are a tech-savvy person who can keep up with the changes in the various algorithms used by those search engines.

No matter what kind of website you run, strategies that entail such natural methods of traffic creation are also a recommended technique because they naturally attract more clients to the goods or services a business offers.

The alternative is to use paid advertising, which is acceptable but does not, in comparison, ensure a long-term conversion rate that is as high as that of organic traffic-building techniques.

This is in addition to the fact that paid advertisements are typically designated as such on the internet, which greatly discourages people from clicking on whatever is presented to them after they know it is an advertisement. This implies that increasing viewer engagement with sponsored advertising requires a lot more effort.

Engaging in search engine optimization is one approach to boost the volume of visitors coming to any website. Whether you look at the stats on a desktop or a mobile device, research has shown that this enhances your website's chances of boosting visitors by 20 times when compared to paid advertising.

In terms of devices, it is crucial to draw that distinction. Later, I'll go into more detail about that.

SEO tactics are not only a useful approach to attract the attention of search engines, but they are also a marketing strategy that pays off over time. The only thing you need to keep in mind is to keep up with the always evolving rules and guidelines established by some of the top names in the search engine industry.

For every piece of content you post on your website, this means making sure the right keywords are included, as they are what search engines utilize to give your page the high position it deserves.

For every particular user query, this ranking significantly affects the order in which search results are displayed. In turn, this offers your website the visibility you want.

Make sure your content is intriguing and pertinent, and you'll discover that something as easy as adding the appropriate keywords will dramatically increase traffic. Paid advertising, in contrast, necessitates ongoing funding and may not always produce the desired outcomes.

However, this goes beyond mere strategy. The first purpose of using the appropriate keywords was to inform search engines about the subject matter of your article and how it should be indexed.

It was a productive approach for search engines like Google to classify your material when a user is looking for relevant data. Although in theory that is still true, there have been a lot more advancements in the field of search engine optimization, and I will cover all of them in this book.

But first, every new company, especially the small and medium-sized ones, must decide whether to hire a professional to complete this portion of the work.

Your willingness to put in the necessary time and effort should be your first priority. It also depends on how intricate a website you plan to manage will be. If it's not a complicated one, you can start by taking care of the essentials yourself.

If you do intend to expand, it won't harm to seek advice from a professional or work with a company to get there. They offer a range of distinct services, each with a varying level of scale and quality. Therefore, before you can decide which is good and appropriate for your activities, you need to know a few things. Later on in this book, I'll go into that as well.

The principles of search engine optimization are among the numerous fundamentals you should be aware of. You must comprehend the criteria used by current search engines like Google and Bing to evaluate your website for this.

Crawlers are used by all search engines to gather data about online material. These crawlers return binary data in the form of 0s and 1s, which the search engine uses to create an index. This index runs your website through a search engine-designed algorithm to see if it fits the user's query.

Making ensuring that the content on the website has all the necessary data and metadata that someone looking for that information is likely to type into the search bar is what is meant by optimizing your website for search engines.

This metadata contains the appropriate title, description, and tags that apply to the associated item. This must be instructive and pertinent. Let's explore that a little more.

**What is SEO**

SEO stands for search engine optimization, as was previously established. When you use SEO, you make sure that both the quantity and quality of the material on your website are directed toward boosting website traffic.

This is done in an effort to increase its visibility and expose your company's brand to as many potential clients as possible. This is a natural method to improve search results for any information you may have.

Because there are so many websites competing for the same audience of online users and because there are trillions of searches made each year, it is an essential component of promoting your product or service online.

Many of these are businesses, and searches play a significant role in how customers discover brands and their products. When you perform well in search engine optimization, the search engines will rank your website higher for specific keywords and key phrases, which will increase the visibility of your brand. This increases your chances of turning a frequent website user into a paying customer.

This isn't as much of a secret now as it was a few years ago. This indicates that companies are getting better at manipulating search engine algorithms to boost the exposure of their websites.

As a result, search engines are continually tightening the screws by altering the criteria by which they rank websites in an effort to give users more meaningful search results rather than giving advantage to companies with poor content. You must therefore constantly be on the lookout for fresh techniques.

Because they rely on advertising for revenue, search engines are also attempting to keep consumers on their search results pages rather than sending them to other websites. This explains why some features are present on the homepage.

Consider this. Ads and organic results can both be found on the SERP, or search engine results page. The highlighted snippet, often known as the answer box, is one such feature. Additionally, there are image carousels that accomplish the same task but just with images. Instead of sending the user to another website, this feature provides a direct response to their query.

Therefore, the user won't only see a list of webpages or be directed to a website that answers the issue if they type "London weather," "convert cm to inches," or "Sydney time now." They see a box with the solution to their query or, in the event of a conversion, a field where they may add the relevant data and instantly receive the results. Similar boxes for queries that can be answered by websites like IMDb and WebMD can also be seen.

By meeting users' demands and keeping them on the SERP pages for a little period of time (which may be confusing, but indicates that the user discovered what he was seeking for quickly), search engines are able to generate revenue more effectively.

Fortunately for businesses, some of this may be legitimately defeated with effective search engine optimization strategies. Both commercial and free content can be used for this. This is how, when a user types a direct query into the search panel, they receive a quick summary of text from the page with the highest rating, which may immediately address the query. This could be an organic outcome from effective SEO.

It takes a little more planning to bring users to your page by avoiding tactics that keep them on the SERP page. Because of this, search engine optimization plays a significant role in many marketing plans developed by both large and small businesses.

At its core, SEO is simply about analyzing the search terms that a potential consumer is using to find your website and figuring out how to use that information to direct them to your website rather than that of your rivals.

Therefore, the core concept is to comprehend your customers. The good news is that the techniques you pick up from search engine optimization don't have to be restricted to your website since it essentially teaches you how to use language more effectively, which can be applied to social media and give your website more traction from social media platforms, which are a significant source of online traffic.

The other aspect of this technique is comprehending what search engine crawlers seek in order to gain visibility. A search engine examines every form of content you have on your website, including texts, images, videos, and other media.

All of this is cataloged, and the two distinct processes of crawling and indexing are used to do so. This indexed data is utilized to assess how pertinent your website's content is to a user's search when they enter a query. Your page is ranked in this manner. Now, the accuracy of keywords is the first thing to be aware of when I discuss ranking. That will be the subject we discuss next.

# Chapter Two

## Researching keywords

When I refer to "keyword research," I'm referring to the words and phrases that your website's content need to contain. This makes it simple for customers looking for this kind of material to locate your website when they enter particular words into the search field.

The goal is to align your knowledge of user preferences with search engine data so that your website will appear at the top of search results when people use those keywords. One of the most crucial components of search engine optimization is this.

Additionally, if you focus on keyword SEO, you will have a better chance of outranking your rivals on the search engine results page. Additionally, when you are conducting a marketing effort, this is quite helpful.

Making a list of keywords that apply to the content you are seeking to optimize is typically the first step in the process. Although it requires time and effort, the results are incredible, making the time and effort entirely worthwhile.

There isn't just one way to achieve this, though. This implies that it will take some trial and error before you get the hang of it. But it's not completely random.

Here are a few things you should not do, for example.

Many people, including some pros, simply look for SEO keywords once and don't periodically update them. Another error is to just use the most well-known keywords, in which case your website will join the many others that have used the same set of keywords.

I mentioned that upgrading keywords is a continuous process. That is because upgrading keywords is similar to maintaining the website's content because, as is obvious, the internet changes frequently and you need to stay up with it. The jargon used by the audience is continuously evolving, therefore you need to stay current.

You need to make sure that the structure is modern whether you are working on a new website or writing for an existing one so that it appeals to potential visitors.

This implies that you need readers to be able to identify the content only by looking at the title and any associated description. This gives them the impression that they are speaking to a real person, albeit a professional one, rather than a machine or an antiquated organization.

As a result, your website will continue to rank highly because consumers will be using these terms when searching. The conclusion is that keyword research is a continuous activity that requires frequent list refinement to remove outdated terms and replace them with more recent ones. To ensure that you don't lose out on visitors from a particular niche, you should always seek for competitive keywords while also including those that are specific.

Another vital aspect of the game that you must work on is diversifying your list of keywords. That is the part about not just using the most well-liked terms. To make sure you can outperform the competition, add the outliers.

There are many internet resources that may assist you in gathering a list of keywords associated with a topic, but you should also do your own research and make sure you keep note of the outcomes of your trial and error methods. In the meanwhile, don't skimp on the content because, in the end, no number of keywords will benefit you if you can't keep your visitors on your site.

Finding out what terms and how popular certain phrases are the main goals of keyword research, which is conducted on virtually every internet user. Teams can study the various ways consumers are researching a certain subject by using this kind of information.

By doing this, you may even create your content around those keywords, such as basing your upcoming blog post on the queries people are typing into a certain search engine.

It's like putting something together to "ride the wave" after noticing a hot hashtag. This practice is referred to as developing tailored content in the industry. And people who come across this information are probably going to spend some time on your website and perhaps even tell their friends and family about your goods and services. They are also more likely to back up their claims with deeds.

In order to understand the psychology of customers, marketers can benefit greatly from keyword research. It explains what is in high demand and how to use a well-known keyword to both improve the content and outperform the competition naturally. Additionally, you discover the language that the group that is most likely to use your products or services speaks.

Now, simply locating the keywords is not sufficient. To achieve the ideal search engine optimization outcomes, you must be aware of the proper order in which to enter them. Finding high-attention or long-tail keywords for your content should be your first order of business. If at all possible, include them in both the title and the text's body.

Additionally, it is strongly advised that you include it in the metadata, such as the picture file names and URLs (which either have the title by default or can be altered if that feature is built in).

However, it's also crucial to keep in mind that some websites contain tens of thousands of keywords. The term for this is keyword density. However, it only makes sense when the quantity of keywords is roughly proportionate to the volume of content on the page.

It's not a good idea to pack your content with too many keywords in a small amount of text, a practice known as keyword stuffing. Search engines are aware of this and disapprove of such tricks. This is due to the fact that relevance is valued above quantity.

Therefore, you must comprehend keyword grouping. This strategy basically involves using a restricted group of pertinent keywords for the content on particular sites.

Here's an illustration, shall we? You could wish to collect all the car-related keywords for the entire segment if you ran an online vehicle magazine. Then, depending on the car brand, you might wish to divide it into smaller portions. By doing this, you can at least somewhat optimize the core elements of all of your pages. Once you've established this process, you may move forward by

1. Add the URL to it.
2. Include it in the website's title.
3. Use its versions in the text's body.
4. Include it in the meta description and tags.
5. Use it for the alt text and file names of images.

Let's now move on to a technique for website optimization that is considerably more in-depth. This entails moving beyond metadata and the micro. Our next chapter is about on-page SEO, which is what this is.

## Chapter Three

## On-Page SEO

The task of optimizing the technical features of the website, some of which we covered in the previous chapter, comes after keyword research and optimization. This process, known as on-page SEO, raises your website's search rankings, boosts traffic, and increases conversion rates. Currently, it takes some time before this practice's effects are seen. So the secret is to be patient.

Both the text and the visual components of the website might benefit from your assistance. The HTML code on the website's back end and the user experience on its front end must both be taken into account. Additionally, there is off-page optimization, which is the work you must do on websites other than your own, such as social media sites and external links. But for now, let's concentrate on the on-page elements.

After keyword research, this is the next critical component of search engine optimization. You can adjust every technical aspect of the website to raise your chances of being ranked highly in search engines.

Now, don't let the technical language frighten you. I'll break it down so you can see that there are only a few changes.

- **Content**

You are aware at this point that you have control over the website's content. In a similar vein, you are responsible for the technical elements as well, not simply the programmers. However, content is where on-page SEO optimization also begins.

Only when the content is helpful to the visitor do they consider a page to be good. For them, it is both the most important and the only thing. Search engines are no different because the user is their top focus. If a search engine does not provide users with pertinent information, it is of little use to them. Therefore, content is crucial for improving rankings as well.

When it comes to SEO, "good content" is material that satisfies user needs and includes a significant number of authority links pointing back to the original source of the data.

This is the same as the idea of supply and demand in international marketplaces. You produce quality content when you meet a significant demand for a particular piece of information, whether it takes the form of text, images, video, or audio.

And when there is likability, that information is given more weight. That implies that you must make it simple for people to link it to their material in order for you to receive traffic from their websites.

What causes this to occur, and how? Nobody connects to a page with poor content because doing so will only irritate their visitors. As a result, when your website is linked within the text of other pages, it's like receiving their approval. In the viewpoint of search engines, this boosts the popularity of your website.

- **Title Tag**

The second important on-page optimization aspect is the title tag. If you're using an outdated website editor, we now move on to the code portion. The majority of website builders today feature simple user interfaces that make it simple to update the title tag of each of your pages, so bear with me and don't worry.

Thus, every webpage's header section has the title tag, an HTML tag. The first contextual element on your website is this. Both the SERP and the window of your browser show it. Although it is not a crucial component for organic ranking on its own, if you mess it up with a poor title tag or a duplicate one, this can undo the progress you have achieved with the other factors.

- **URL**

The arrangement of the categories on your website is the next aspect of on-page SEO to take into account after internal linking. Here's an illustration to help.

If your website's address is anything like https://www.websitename.com/USnews/washington.. It's a nice one because it covers general US news before focusing on Washington specifically. This data is used by search engines to assess the relevance of a web page.

The hierarchy aids in the indexing of the pages by the search engines, which in turn aids in the listing of the pages for individuals who are especially looking for, say, local Washington news. And before it even looks at the content, this occurs. Therefore, the hierarchy of URLs is crucial.

In contrast, a URL that appears arbitrary, such as https://www.websitename/report/washington17254..., does not convey a hierarchy and is of little use to search engines. Additionally, it is unable to categorize the page because no one will really search for the terms "report" and "washington17254" on the page. Since that is one of the simplest things you could have done, your URL has no meaning to the search engine. It was a chance lost.

- **Meta Description**

The meta description is another element that has been crucial since the beginning of SEO. On the search engine results page, the description that appears immediately beneath the title of your page is this. It is crucial since it provides the user with a glimpse into the information on your website.

There is some evidence to suggest that these descriptions are helpful, though not as much as they used to a decade ago when it comes to Google results. If you think of yourself as a lazy search engine user who doesn't bother opening several pages to see what they're about, you'll see the value that meta descriptions add.

It is well recognized that having strong meta descriptions can help with things like click-through rate, or CTR, and perceptions of the quality of your website.

- **Headlines**

The optimization of websites for search engines also includes this. You would be astonished at how many websites entirely disregard keyword research for this feature. A decent headline for your blog posts may seem like an easy solution.

In addition to generating user interest, a strong title can help you stand out on the search engine results page. You are aware of what we're talking about if you are familiar with the idea of clickbait.

However, they will probably think you are crying wolf, which will injure you more in the long run!

- **User Experience**

The issue of user experience on the front end is the last one. The majority of users are likely to be non-technical individuals who would like to be able to locate what they are looking for immediately or at least reasonably easily.

Recognize that nobody enjoys giving a new website—one they haven't visited before—the benefit of the doubt. Because internet users are notoriously impatient, it is your responsibility to make the website simple to use.

This calls for a straightforward design, engaging colors, and a visually appealing website. If you accomplish that, you will have a starting point.

# Chapter Four
## Link Building

Google is undoubtedly the first name that comes to mind when you consider optimizing the content on your website for search engines. And with good reason. More so than search engines like Bing and Yahoo, the tech giant considers links a lot of weight when determining a website's rating. Links are a wonderful way for search engines to determine the value of a web page and discover further material.

As was previously indicated, from the perspective of search engines, links pointing to a website within the content of other websites are similar to good reviews. Like saying they believe in your material enough to send some of their visitors your way. Therefore, every website must create a strong link profile.

But over time, businesses became overly clever about this and overused this by posting their links on forums and spamming the comments sections of other websites.

Because these kinds of links are merely links for the sake of it and aren't actually helpful to the users of any website, it forced search engines to investigate more carefully to identify inorganic patterns.

However, link building is still crucial; you just need to make sure that the website's visitors can understand them. To achieve this, make sure your links are the following:

1. Beneficial to website visitors
2. Naturally situated
3. Provide the user with high-quality, pertinent material
4. Feature quality anchor text

**Comparing good and bad links**

Let's first examine the differences between a good link and a bad link from the perspective of a search engine before examining the various ways that link development will aid in SEO. These are the elements.

#1. The Authority of the Web Page

You must look for websites that will reference your work via links. But it's crucial that those websites have authoritative voices. Search engines evaluate the linking's quality in this way. For instance, receiving a link back from the Wall Street

Journal or New York Times is much more significant than receiving one from an unknown blogger.

#2. Relevance of the Website

The next consideration after a website's authority that links back to your content is its relevancy to your content. If you run a sports website, a backlink from an expert on the subject is worth much more than one from a forum with no connection to sports. You must therefore choose websites that have a close connection to your content, goods, or services.

#3. The location of the link on the page

You also need to figure out a strategy to ensure that the link is incorporated high up in the body of their article and not at the bottom as an afterthought after you have a voice of authority referring back to you for relevant material.

A key component of connecting is the location of the link. There is less value in something in the footer or sidebar than there is at the start or center of the material.

#4. Editorial Positioning

After determining the location, you must determine if the words to which the hyperlink is associated qualify as editorial links. The link is put editorially if it causes their visitors to get interested in your content. It is not editorial linking if it is positioned arbitrarily without reference to your link.

For search engines like Google, editorial links are much more valuable than links that are randomly put. Non-editorial links may even be viewed as unnatural links, which Google may view as a breach of their criteria and perhaps punish you for.

#5. The Anchor Text for the Link

You learn a new term in this book. The area of the link that can be clicked is called the "anchor text" in this scenario. The anchor text of a link is taken carefully by search engines, particularly Google, and is also used as a factor in determining how highly your website will be ranked. Additionally, websites have exploited this technique improperly over time. Therefore, if your anchor text contains a lot of terms, it can be viewed as spam.

**Hyperlinks and Search Engines**

In essence, search engines like to use two sorts of links to determine a website's rating. The first sort of links aids in finding new information, and the second kind aids in a website's ranking in a search engine. After the web pages are crawled and their content is extracted for indexing, this choice is made.

The search engine is prepared to rank the page after it is satisfied that the linking satisfies the aforementioned requirements and has the appropriate selection of keywords. As we now know, the choice extends beyond the page's content.

The value of your website is determined by looking at the links to external websites and evaluating those websites. Your website's chances of appearing higher on the search engine results page rise as you are able to acquire more links from high-value websites.

But if you overlink without being careful, Google will probably penalize you for over-optimization. On the other hand, developing low-quality links is a waste of time because it has no impact on how likely it is for your website to rank highly if the websites connecting back to your content are not of good quality. Finding a balance between the quantity of backlinks and the caliber of people who are connecting to you is therefore necessary.

Not to mention, your website is likely to receive a lot of traffic from high-quality backlinks.

## Chapter Five

How to Implement a Content Marketing Strategy

There aren't many discussions regarding content marketing when it comes to business SEO. This error is made by several professionals as well. You will, however, understand better after reading this chapter.

Content marketing is a crucial component of contemporary marketing, along with SEO. If these two ideas are combined and executed well, you can create a website that is unstoppable.

Your brand will be able to get the most out of any digital campaign if you develop a content marketing plan and keep SEO in mind. Because they combine two potent ideas, these kinds of methods are frequently referred to as integrated strategies.

## When Content Marketing and SEO Collide

In today's world, social media is a vital component of daily life for both individuals and organizations. Businesses spend a lot of time and money promoting their goods and services on websites like Facebook, Twitter, Instagram, and other social media channels because their target audiences are there.

Another aspect of internet marketing that shows promise is email marketing. They don't guarantee that they will always reach the target audience, though. This sort of integrated marketing plan can help with that.

As an illustration, when a user of a certain product or service has a query, they immediately go to a search engine and type it into the search bar. Then, search engines like Google locate a website that has the answer to that query.

By making your content more effective, you have a chance to directly address that group of potential clients. Giving them the appropriate information at the appropriate moment is the goal here. That is how content marketing and search engine optimization work together to strengthen your brand.

**The Method of Execution**

It only requires a few easy actions. You will be able to fully profit once you have put them in place. This is how it goes.

Step 1: Identify your audience.

The goal of content optimization is to make it simple for users to find the goods or services they need. Therefore, you must begin by figuring out who these clients are. When you accomplish that, you will be able to provide the type of material customers require. Additionally, you may tap into their searches and capture their interest by making it SEO-friendly. By asking and answering a few straightforward questions, you can do that.

You must determine who your current clientele is. Knowing who they are can help you find information about their preferences and additional expectations for your brand. Both qualitative and quantitative data are included in this type. Research age, gender, past purchases, and customer interaction with your website or brand. This offers you a general idea of who your typical existing customer is.

Finding out who your competitors are is the following data point. Look at your competition to determine what your demographic wants and why they choose certain businesses. Customers' evaluations and comments on reputable blogs, as well as social media accounts, almost immediately provide this information.

Customers that are satisfied with the competition help you identify any weaknesses you may have. You can determine if there is a gap in the market you can fill when you locate customers that are dissatisfied with the competition.

This brings up the question of what you may provide to entice clients away from your rivals' brands. This calls for you to consider the goods and services you currently provide and the target market who benefits from them. You can find openings by combining that with the data you've already obtained about your rivals.

In conclusion, comprehend the market value of your brand. Learn what the opinions of your current and prospective clients are regarding your services and goods. Find out what you need to improve on as well as your strong points. You can acquire this information by conducting brief surveys on social media or your own website.

You can develop your buyer persona and segment your consumer base using the responses to all of these questions. Now that you can create content that is tailored to this audience and optimize it for search engines, you can communicate with them more successfully and increase traffic to your website. If the content is strong, you can persuade them to make a purchase or increase their level of loyalty among current clients.

Step 2: Define who you are.
You are aware of your audience and their needs. You may or may not already be aware of the competitors and what they have to offer. You have the ability to (re)define your brand because of this.

Find out what people are talking about right now, then make content about those issues. Make sure you convey your knowledge of the subject with authority. Spend resources on it even if it means doing extra effort and research since the end product will be fantastic in the long term. Additionally, the information you offer must be original and not a repeat of something else. Make an effort to be distinctive with your views as well as your language.

Step 3: Conduct a keyword analysis
You are aware of the main issue here.

Step 4: Produce Excellent Content

Take the material outside of your blogs once you've identified the distinctive content themes and the keywords that will enable you to connect with your target audience. Adding lengthy content like white papers and ebooks to the website may even be something you want to think about doing. An important component of SEO is video content. If you haven't already, you should consider starting to invest there.

Now, you need to go beyond keywords if you want your customers to stay on your page and investigate what you have to offer. Your research on developing original content subjects will be useful in this situation.

Produce fantastic content that search engines and consumers will both value. By doing this, you also avoid search engine penalties for poor content. Here's how to improve your material beyond the obvious idea, which is a genuine stroke of genius.

1. Make sure there are no grammatical or spelling mistakes in your blog postings. That sort of behavior detracts from your image as a genuine candidate. Make sure the

components are properly structured so that they flow from one idea to the next.

2. To make your theory simpler to understand, include examples.
Avoid using words that the common reader would not comprehend, such as technical jargon. If you do use such language, give readers a brief explanation or, if it's an ebook, include a glossary.
Additionally, it improves how people relate to your brand.

3. Make sure to speak in their language if you are aware of your audience's demographics. Be friendly but not ridiculous. Use a conversational tone so that they won't think they are reading material that has been churned out by a machine.

4. Ensure that the content is properly structured. Use brief paragraphs and bullet points to keep the reader from getting bored.

For those who are only skimming the page, periodically summarize the main parts of the plot.

Step 5: Update Your Content in Step

The last stage is to continue playing the content game. By updating content that is still relevant years after it was written, this is made possible. You are aware of the value of changing headlines, descriptions, keywords, and tags. Check to see if there is anything you can add to the content to make it more current. In addition, here are some options for you.

1. Add interesting details or figures to make it more impactful.
2. Adapt the metadata to your preferred search engine
3. Check the website traffic numbers and occasionally evaluate the material.

Basically, if a blog post remains popular weeks or months after it was written, make sure to capitalize on the traffic it is receiving by updating it and taking advantage of any relevant trends.

## Chapter Six

### 10 SEO Best Practices for Website

White hat SEO and black hat SEO are two terms that you will frequently hear while talking about appropriate SEO strategies. Don't let the language scare you. These are two fundamentally distinct ideas.

White hat strategies are ones that work to improve your website's reputation with search engines using ethical practices that really strive to supply users with high-quality material, which leads to better search engine ranks.

In essence, black hat methods are the opposite. You raise moral issues and run the risk of being penalized by search engines when you use cheap tricks to trick the search engine.

Fortunately, these definitions are not made at random. Furthermore, these fines must be handled seriously because they have immediate effects on business. Shortcuts are convenient and enticing in the short term, but the risk is excessive, and, to be honest, it is not worth it.

Techniques used in "black hat" SEO include keyword stuffing and link scraping. Along with receiving severe penalties, you also run the risk of getting blacklisted, which is the removal from search results.

#1. Position for Keywords

When you have a solid set of keywords, it makes sense to employ them more frequently in order to increase traffic to your content. Although you already know not to go overboard, you still need to make sure the important keyword is at the top of the page. This is so that Google can see the most important keywords right away, such in the first line.

#2. Search Intent

The phrase "search" or "user intent" also evaluates the motivation behind each user inquiry. This is a top goal for Google because, when they understand the context in which a person is searching, they can identify websites that provide the information they're looking for. So, if you want to appear on the top search results page, you must also succeed in this. There are four categories into which this can be categorized.

1. Information: This frequently entails providing the consumer with a direct response to a brief and focused question.

2. When a person searches a website for a product or service, they are using navigation. A excellent example is "Twitter login". It only requires locating the login page.

3. Businesses: This occurs when a user searches for a product but decides not to purchase it just yet. "Best of" lists for that particular category are frequently the outcome of this.

4. Transactions: This occurs when a user is prepared to make a purchase and searches for a tool to help them do so.

A good example is "Buy iPhone 6s".

You have an advantage over the competition if you comprehend the user's motivations for their search.

#3. Page Speed

The speed at which your website loads is crucial for both user ease and search engine optimization.

It wasn't always like this, but in the current market, if your page loads slowly, your users will leave like they're on fire.

Such pages are not something that search engines like to suggest to their visitors.

According to data, even a one-second delay might cause a conversion rate loss of 7%. Additionally, data reveals that when a website takes longer than three seconds to load, about 40% of visitors depart.

Businesses are now becoming more careful about how their websites are constructed. Additionally, search engine optimization significantly affects how much money is made. Thus, page speed becomes important. This can be accomplished by removing heavy and unnecessary page elements, such as plugins.

#4. Utilize HTTPS

If you didn't know it already, HTTPS increases the security of your website. This is due to the fact that when your website is secured with the HTTPS protocol, the data exchange between the server and the user is encrypted. This can be confirmed by checking the URL in the loading bar of the browser to see if a lock icon is there.

Since 2014, it has grown in significance for Google SEO rankings. If the lock icon is missing, you will need to purchase an SSL certificate, which is readily available from many web servers. All pages will need to have it installed, but you just need to do it once.

#5. Prevent Duplicate Content

When discussing the importance of maintaining original material on your website, I briefly touched on this. However, Google looks for this. It is extremely evident that the website shouldn't have any material that is identical or nearly identical on different pages.

In other words, it's against the law to copy content from your own work. The title tags, product pages, landing pages, meta descriptions, alternative text for pictures, and other content components are all examples of where this is true.

It's not a hard rule to comprehend. Simply said, it means that all of the content must be original. It can be a little challenging if you manage a big website with plenty of goods and services. But if you put enough effort into the writing, you can handle it. If there is so much overlap in the material, you might also consider combining pages.

#6. Optimize Your Images

A wonderful method to break up text on a page is to include graphics. However, if they are not optimized, they may take a very long time to load and may even slow down the pace of the entire page. You are once again faced with a poor user experience. The images you chose for the information you wrote clearly took a lot of your time. Just be sure to take some extra time to optimize them utilizing some tried-and-true industry tricks.

#7 Add Useful Links

I've talked about building links, which is when other websites point to your material. However, you might want to consider doing the same. It is common to believe that it might cause visitors to leave your page. However, it is a crucial element of an SEO strategy.

You provide the visitor with reliable information when you link back to authoritative pages that contain pertinent information. This improves the information on your website and raises its search engine rating.

You can anticipate reciprocation when you produce content that is beneficial or pertinent to their website because it demonstrates some level of trust between the two websites. For instance, if you reciprocate when a blogger links back to your website, you can anticipate a higher outcome.

This is not about exchanging favors; rather, it is about utilizing the data on each other's websites to raise their Google ranks and provide users with the information they need.

When you produce quality material, you can even receive a shoutout from these authoritative websites if you have enough goodwill.

#8. Conduct Keyword Research

You are aware of the significance of this in ensuring that a search engine can find your website. Use the phrases that your current and potential customers use to find your products and services if you want to produce content that gets consumed.

To avoid being buried among the thousands of other websites utilizing the exact same set of keywords, make sure you are looking at both high-volume keywords and terms that make you stand out from the competition.

Verify the search volume for the keywords you choose, which can provide you with an approximation of the traffic to each of them.

#9. The Google Search Console

This is an excellent method of learning how well your website is doing on the search engine results page. This is highly beneficial for SEO and functions as a dashboard for your website. Reports on three of the most important criteria are among its many features.

1. Performance: This information includes the number of times your URL is clicked when it appears in the Google SERP, as well as the keywords they utilized and the position you were given on the page. Additionally, you will learn about clicks and impressions, which let you know if your SEO strategy is effective.

2. Improvement: This relates to usability on mobile. This component of the report provides information on how you are doing when using a mobile device, which accounts for a sizable portion of all internet usage. Additionally, since

Google bases its indexing on mobile-first criteria, it's important to understand how you rank in this area.

3. Coverage: This informs you of the number of Google indexed pages on your website. In order for you to resolve the issue, it informs you whether it is unable to crawl any of those pages and why. By taking immediate action, you increase your chances of appearing higher on Google's SERP.

#10. Long-Form Content

Because fewer people are reading long-form information than they would like, this has fallen out of favor. However, the reality is that long-form material has a better probability of moving up the Google results page. Numerous studies have demonstrated that long-format articles with a word count of more than 3,000 are the best performers.

In comparison to articles that are between 900 and 1,200 words in length, these are likely to receive three times as much traffic, four times as many shares, and 3.5 times as many backlinks. It is important to consider how the length of the material affects search performance.

Therefore, you might wish to have at least a few of these pieces that are thoroughly researched and include essential information presented in a friendly manner without using jargon.

**Chapter Seven**

Advance Tactics

A strategy to enter the game and remain there is to learn about best practices. But over time, you must expand on those insights in order to advance and surpass the competition when it comes to managing digital advertising. To do that, you'll need to use a few cutting-edge tactics. Your starter package for that is right here.

1 - Create Topic Clusters

This relates to a collection of materials developed from a central idea. As subcategories, you make a variety of themes and connect to the page with the primary theme. This means that you have a single overarching topic with numerous subtopics so that people who are interested in that issue can browse your site for a longer time to gather all the information. Additionally, it gives you the option to group these articles together as similar themes.

Because you may produce a lot of information as a voice of authority that is pertinent to the user, topic clusters are a terrific method to optimize the content on your website. It resembles the reverse of one long-format composition in some ways.

You can also give the customer the impression that you are covering a variety of topics and persuade them that you are an authority on the subject by writing five or six pieces on the same subject from various angles.

2 - Perform an SEO Audit

Auditing your website is one more approach to boost SEO. This clarifies how sales and search traffic are related. You can engage professionals to assist you, but if you comprehend the fundamental principles, you should be able to handle it on your own.

An organized technique to comprehend a subject or an event is through an audit. This term is frequently connected to financial matters, but it also exists in the SEO industry. It assists you in retaining your current clients while drawing in new ones.

When you conduct an SEO audit, you evaluate the overall performance of your website, set goals, and plan for the future. By filling in any holes or flaws with the current information on your website, this helps you enhance your income.

Usually, you find out about the issues with your titles and descriptions that are frequently ignored. That is a serious error. What you perform during an SEO audit is as follows.

Ensure that the names and descriptions of every piece of content are optimized.

Ensure the article contains the appropriate keywords while staying away from keyword stuffing.

Ensure that your URL is clear and correctly formatted so that the search engine can understand what the web page is about.

Ensure that the headings and subheadings are used to format the content and other page elements. At least two to three sentences should be in each paragraph. Italics or bold must be used for important words. A call to action should always be included.

Add photos, optimize them, and give each one an alt attribute.

Include dependable, pertinent links in the text. Both internal and external connections are included.

3 – Look for Journalist Keywords

These are the search terms that journalists use to find information. I don't want to bust your bubble, but writers frequently search Google for particular numbers to add to their articles.

You greatly increase the likelihood that backlinks to your website from their articles will occur when you choose the keywords they are most likely to employ. You receive a link back from a high-quality website when a journalist from a reputable publication takes notice of your content.

When they cite their source, they would also enjoy the internet traffic. This provides them with motivation. Win-win situation.

4 - Internal Linking Work

You can benefit from using this underutilized SEO strategy. Links pointing to content on your own website let search engines know that you have more, useful content available. This is a chance for the search engine to find fresh information, which plays a significant role in how highly it ranks your website.

Your chances of being found on the SERP increase when your internal linking strategy is robust and your search engine indexing improves. This is a natural technique to increase visibility, and by using the appropriate anchor text, it becomes much more effective. Apply this consistently to all of your content.

5 - Use dynamic parameters

Your site pages must be easy for search engines to crawl in order for them to be properly indexed. Therefore, you must employ pagination, a method of distributing your content over a number of pages. Typically, this is done to separate products on e-commerce websites.

As an illustration, if your website's existing URL is https://websitename.com/sports-topics/page/5

You desire it to be formatted like
https://websitename.com/athletics-topics.page=5

This enables Google to recognize your paginated URLs and prevents it from repeatedly indexing the same pages. This expedites indexing and brings you one step closer to rising in the rankings more quickly.

## Chapter Eight

Measuring and Tracking SEO Results

You must monitor the effectiveness of your SEO techniques, whether you use Google Analytics (which is advised) or some other tool. This offers you the chance to determine which strategies work best for your content and what needs to be done to fix the ineffective ones.

Do you need to change it, drop it, or completely change course?

Data analysis holds the key to resolving these issues.

Again, you can pay an SEO specialist to explain it to you; but, it is not that tough. To help you understand what you're looking at, let's offer you a tutorial on the key indicators that show you how your strategies are performing.

1 - Organic Traffic

Finding out how you are doing in terms of organic search traffic from search engines is the first step. These are the outcomes a user receives after entering a certain string of characters in the search field.

The first thing to find out is how many people are visiting your website as a result of this. This is as a result of its targeting. They have a specific question, and if you can provide the answer, you ought to be ranked highly enough to meet their needs. You have a good possibility of landing a paying client if you achieve here. Due to your strong visibility, this also implies that your whole organic strategy is effective.

2 - SEO Traffic Quality

Checking the rise or fall in the conversion rate is the greatest way to establish if the traffic you are receiving is quality traffic or not. This means that you must check to see if visitors to your website are actually purchasing your goods or services.

Are they becoming paying clients if they are new users? You can use a number of techniques to find out if and when this is happening.

To determine whether things are getting better or worse, you may also compare the numbers from this week or month to the prior one. Additionally, you can find out if someone made any purchases as a result of multiple visits.

If your overall traffic is stable but your conversion rate declines, your traffic may not be of good quality. Because it indicates that visitors are coming to the site but not making a purchase of your goods or services.

On the other hand, you can claim that you are receiving high-quality traffic if you make a change, such as beginning to focus on keywords, and you notice an improvement in the conversion rate.

3 - Keyword Ranking

Once your website has been optimized, you will be able to monitor the progress for long-tail and targeted keywords. By performing a quick Google search using those terms, you can accomplish this. Your best chance of success is to be on the first page of the SERP, which is what 25% of users click on.

Analyzing keyword gaps is another option. You are provided with competitor URLs and the keywords that are effective for them.

You can correct your own keyword list with this. It's a fantastic approach to reach a group of people you may not have previously engaged.

4 - Find pages that Take Long to Load

This is sometimes overlooked, but if you check how long it takes for your webpages to load, you'll see if it's something you should focus on. You lose the game if it takes the page more than 1-3 seconds.

Additionally, as previously indicated, page speed plays a significant role in Google results. When you look at the analytics, this is frequently displayed as a separate entity because it is a crucial one.

A decent tool will provide metrics for different devices so you can focus on each one separately. The programmers can then review this to see what needs to be done to optimize the page.

5 - Engagement Metrics

You can learn a lot about user behavior through stats. Here are a few well-known ones.

1. Time on Page, also known as Dwell Time, is the length of time visitors stay on a specific webpage. You can tell they are not reading a long-form article if they are only spending a very brief amount of time with it.

However, it's not so bad if they only take a few seconds to read a "about me" page. So pay attention to the subject and the appropriate moment.

2. Pages per Visit: Knowing how many pages a visitor has read lets you gauge how interesting the content is. Therefore, you can adjust the content as necessary.

Or just leave things alone.

3. Bounce Rate: This is the percentage of visitors who leave a page empty-handed. It lets you know whether or not visitors think the content's quality to be interesting. But keep in mind that it says nothing about their experience.

Because users are not accustomed to the new layout, often when websites are improved and rebuilt, the bounce rate rises before it falls.

So, read the data carefully, but also apply your own discretion to interpret what the results mean.

# Summary

The SEO-related facts you might not know could fill an entire book! It is true, though. So first of all, congrats on finishing the article. I've made an effort to include all the factors in this book that lead a search engine to favor your website. By what every type of website can benefit from SEO, and the basics have already been covered.

Additionally, you have learnt a lot about vocabulary and the difference between ethical and unethical behavior. You are aware of the consequences for abiding by the rules as well as the benefits of doing so.

Also, you have learnt about shortcuts and why it is wise to stay away from them. Even more sophisticated strategies have been examined, along with how easily they might be used.

Now, a lot of this may be delegated to experts who are knowledgeable about the tools needed to complete all of this and more swiftly and effectively.

However, if you have the time to handle this internally, you may direct those resources toward the more imaginative tasks that form the core of your business.

When you get that desired high placement on SERPs, you attract a lot of attention and may even win over lifelong customers. And that material is frequently impossible to purchase, not even through paid promotion.

## Three Important Off-Page SEO Techniques

If a website owner wants to increase the visibility of his or her website in search engine results, on-page search engine optimization is unquestionably one of the most important techniques.

On-page SEO, however, frequently calls for technical expertise. Why? HTML fans are a small minority. To optimize web pages effectively, this is frequently what needs to be changed.

What if a geek friend previously completed the on-page optimization and you're wondering how you may improve your website's "search engine goodness"? Next up is off-page optimization.

You'll have to wish for one-way backlinks as the outcome. Why? Many of the main search engines, including Google, Yahoo!, and MSN, rank webpages in this way. The more backlinks from relevant, high-page-ranking websites, the better.

So how do you actually collect backlinks? If you're not the techie kind, it's not a simple chore, but it's surely less nerve-wracking than HTML. Off-page SEO advice is provided below:

## 1. Article Promotion

It has been determined that high-quality content reigns supreme. People are ravenous for up-to-date, high-quality information, therefore by making it available, backlinks will proliferate. Being a talented writer is really helpful in achieving success in this pursuit. Additionally, get comfortable with resource box usage. Only websites with content pertinent to the articles you submit to article directories should be listed.

## 2. Participation in forums

Find forums with topics that relate to the information on your website, and maintain sharing knowledge that the forum participants will find useful. Your off-page SEO effort will be successful if you use your signature or the tag-along message that appears at the end of each of your postings. Ensure that it delivers information about your website while being straightforward. To make it simple for those who want to visit your site, learn how to hyperlink.

3. Blogging

The most used tools by SEO specialists today are blogs and online logs. In addition to being simple to update, they don't call for a too formal tone, which many readers prefer. Blogs are kept current and search engine friendly by an informal dialogue that can be achieved by readers leaving comments and the blog owner responding to the remarks. The search engines will remain aware of your website if you continue to write a blog that is once again pertinent to the content of your website. Don't forget to provide a link from your blog to your primary website.

Consistency is the key to using these off-page SEO techniques successfully. A certain strategy to make your website stand out is to consistently produce content for your own blog and submit high-quality articles to websites at least two to three times per week. In order to increase the popularity of your website with search engines and to get knowledge from other forum users' participation, you should participate in forums more frequently. Additionally, if you find that you don't like doing these things, you can always hire someone to do them for you as a backup plan!

## 4 Steps to Improve Search Engine Positioning For Law Firm Website

Well, by this point, you've probably heard that achieving top search engine placement requires a number of factors, including effective key word density, user-friendly navigation, accurate Meta tags, high-quality incoming connections, and useful content. When it comes to legal firm websites, this is especially true. One of the most competitive categories for search engine ranking optimization efforts is the legal search engine rankings.

For the purposes of this post, I'll assume that your legal website already shines in the aforementioned areas and that your site has a respectable reputation for the legal search phrases you want to target.

However, as you are well aware, the Internet can produce quality clients at a much lower cost than any other media. Therefore, upgrading your legal website should be a really good choice.

I've listed several incredibly successful suggestions for raising your search engine rankings below:

1. Find a different legal website!

Yes, at approximately $53 a month for the first year. You can have a second website for $11 per month beginning in the second year.

A legal website would cost you about $500 to create, $10 to register a new domain name for a year, and $10 a month for high-quality hosting for the first year. Due to a decrease in the site creation charge in the second year, the cost decreases.

There shouldn't be any visual or editorial similarities between your second site and your first one. If you don't follow this, major search engines may stop referring to your website.

Your webpages should each focus on a separate practice area while being about your company. Additionally, links between the two of your websites are required.

2. Choose a URL

You need a web address for your new website. Choose a domain name for your new legal website that includes a few of your search phrases. Which website, www.smith-

smithandklein.com or www.sandiegolawyerforyou.com, do you believe would receive more search engine traffic?

Even if you have a strong local reputation, a potential client looking for a San Diego lawyer is more likely to find the first site than the second. As a result, adding keywords to your URL will improve your visibility in key word searches.

3. Invest in website development tools.

As the website's owner, you or your helper should be able to keep it current by adding fresh information or making little adjustments. To keep your website current, updating should be done frequently. HTML knowledge is not required due to the abundance of free and inexpensive web site applications. I believe that the greatest option for website development software is Microsoft FrontPage.

4. Get educated on SEO by reading a book.

The power of knowledge. The majority of the time, website designers are excellent at creating websites but terrible at optimization. If they do attempt optimization, they frequently do so using out-of-date strategies that, in many cases, have resulted in sites ranking far below their full potential or being banned due to what is viewed as search engine manipulation.

Become the ruler of your territory rather than its serf! Read a book on search engine optimization now!

## The Top 5 SEO Considerations

A website's visibility on search engine radars is achieved by a technique known as search engine optimization, or SEO. Being found when a potential consumer conducts a search on Google or Yahoo is essential given that there are more than 4 billion publicly accessible websites on the Internet. There is very little chance that a potential customer will find your website if it does not appear on the first few pages of results.

When beginning your SEO journey, do not anticipate seeing results right away. Similar to cheese, a website's search engine ranking improves over time. There was no need to optimize the website for search engines to find it in the early days of the internet.

A robot, sometimes known as a search spider, could visit every website on the Internet back then in a matter of hours.

Today's websites are measured in petabytes (PB), the unit of data storage after terabytes, and it takes search engines at least 72 hours to crawl and index all of the pages.

It's all about setting up the elements a website needs to be search engine friendly. Every page on the website needs to have purposeful title and description text to start.

Additionally, it requires that a list of potential keywords have been thoroughly investigated, with the relevant ones having been chosen. After that, link exchanges must be set up and submissions must be made to search engine queues.

Spend the time to research the organization before deciding to hire someone to handle the SEO for your website. Here are some inquiries to make:

1. Does the business have any prior SEO experience?

2. What ranking does their website have on Google and Yahoo? What are the possibilities that they will succeed with your site if they are unable to optimize their own?

3. What plan do they have for your website? While the majority of SEO agencies won't go into specifics about HOW they would carry out SEO, they ought to be able to outline WHAT they have in mind for your website.

4. Will the SEO company blast-submit your site to the search engines using an automatic software or manually? Blasting a website is quicker and less expensive, but there are drawbacks. Among them are

a. Search engines for pornographic material may submit your website.
b. As some search engines view blast-submission as a form of spam, they either remove these entries from their directories or prevent them from being entered via CAPTCHA (a challenge-response test used in computing to determine whether the user is human) in the first place. As a result, your site might not be allowed to be listed.
c. A "link-farm" may submit your website.

5. A minimum of three months is required to notice any difference in search engine position. Due to the aging algorithm used by most Search Engines, it will usually take

between 6 and 8 months! Ask the following inquiries if the business "guarantees" the top spot on search engines:

a. Are they going to utilize pay-per-click or pay-per-keyword to boost your website to the top of the search results? While both approaches are acceptable, they are quite expensive and only a temporary replacement for effective SEO techniques.
b. Is the person you hired Larry Page, the man behind Google? Since nobody else will be able to provide such a guarantee.

A novice SEO specialist may do more harm than good to the site's ranking. If your website goes into a negative area, you as the site owner will ultimately have to deal with the search engines.

## 12 SEO-Related Facts You Must Know

According to studies, more than 90% of all online users utilize search engines to find the information or goods/services they're looking for.

I believe that the following twelve points will highlight a sound and efficient attitude, approach, and methodology to the SEO question as well as provide some valuable insight into the business itself.

1. Content. Content. Content.
Copywriting that is efficient, professional, and optimized is the single, most crucial element in any SEO strategy. Websites are indexed by search engines depending on the content of each page.

One can move a website to the high echelons of the "SERP's" (Search Engine Results Pages) in a methodical and ethical way with a solid understanding of the language and grammatical rules paired with diligent study to locate and exploit the market focus.

2. Review web logs.
At least twice measure everything before rechecking. I'll be the first to admit that many of the techniques used in website optimization are more art than science, but the outcomes of the work require a very scientific approach.

This is accomplished by meticulously compiling and examining the web logs of the sites. Although there is a variety of specialist software that can help with the task, keeping a tight check on site visitors and their activity while they are there is still necessary.

No matter how carefully a strategy is thought out, it remains mainly theoretical unless it is supported by the outcomes, which can only be determined by the logs and a careful examination of their contents.

3. Nobody can promise that their website will rank #1 on Google or any other search engine.
They are either making a false claim that they have no intention of keeping, or they have an inside edge at Google, which they will quickly lose when the honest Google employees find out about it.

Those who make such claims will either optimize for such nebulous search term phrases that no one will likely ever look for (such as "green stunted widgets with purple Polka-dots and icing") or they are making a false claim that they have no intention of keeping. I should also highlight the alternative possibility—that they will simply take the money and flee—but I'll be courteous.

4. Some things are merely ridiculous.

Your website doesn't have to be submitted to 50,000 search engines. Businesses who provide this service are, at best, dubious. One search engine, which generates 85% of all Internet search results, will find your website just fine on its own if you have one link from a reputable website or, even better, a directory. Over 90% of all web traffic is accounted for by only four (4) search engines. Regarding any purported advantage that would result from being featured in a niche Botswana search engine that focuses on safaris to the Kalahari Desert and gets 7 hits per day, well, you figure it out.

5. Pay-per-Click is not SEO.

The effectiveness of increasing traffic and sales through a well-planned pay-per-click campaign is undeniable, but the conversion rates are typically poor and end as soon as the "pay" is stopped.

While results may take a little longer with a well-planned and carried out SEO campaign, they continue to produce, and in fact develop, even after the work is finished and paid for. After a site has undergone extensive optimization, we frequently discover that only modest adjustments are required on an ongoing basis, primarily in relation to fresh content and/or new products or services.

6. SEO is neither shamanism, Druidism, nor witchcraft.
It also doesn't call for any unique chants, ritual fires, or garb, though some of us do occasionally like howling during the full moon.

There are no "Top Secret" techniques that an ethical SEO cannot discuss with a customer, a judge, or even his mother. With a significant investment of time and money, anything about SEO may be learned because of the cooperative nature of the Internet itself.

A reputable SEO company will provide you with a breakdown of each expense component. If you detect a clandestine environment or a reluctance to provide information, proceed with caution. While some technical details may require some previous knowledge to properly comprehend, if one has a good understanding of the complete scenario, it should be simple to come up with an explanation.

7. Do SEO yourself.

You can develop and coordinate your own SEO strategy, or you can hire a respectable SEO company to do it for you. After discussing the objectives of the business or website, conducting an in-depth website analysis, researching a wide range of search terms, and receiving focused instruction on the best practices for achieving high SERPs, about half of my own clients either do some of the actual work themselves or delegate it to internal staff members who are dedicated to the task.

These first steps are then followed by a comprehensive program of recommendations and techniques, which the client can either carry out themselves or contract out to others. 30–40% on average in savings.

8. Implementation in phases.

While many businesses invest thousands of dollars each month on search engine optimization, there is an alternative that will benefit you in terms of more sales and leads without the significant upfront cost.

The most crucial factor is to have a trustworthy company handle the first examination and proposed optimization strategies.

Long-term costs of the trial-and-error approach are significantly higher, whether or not the desired outcome is achieved. You can put the strategy into action as soon as finances permit after analyzing it and creating a manageable budget.

9. It's a good idea to keep in mind the adage, "If it sounds too good to be true, it probably is."

This has never been more true than in the world of SEO. While a carefully planned and implemented optimization approach will always produce tangible and quantifiable benefits, the Internet is a cutthroat media and we all strive to be at the top. Accept that a slow, steady ascent over time will put you well ahead of a flash and crash.

10. A thing to think about.
Your website, your company, and perhaps even your reputation are on the line in the race for the top. Avoid using any "shortcuts" or unethical tactics suggested by anyone to

further your company objectives. All things considered, you, the business owner, are ultimately accountable for any firm or person you hire.

Demand to be informed in detail about the strategy and the actions being taken to implement it.

Ask for and receive an explanation if anything even remotely seems strange. In this situation, ignorance is not just not bliss; it may also be the beginning of the end for your company.

11. Not every incoming link is created equal.
The importance of an inbound link to your own PR ranking depends on its relevancy to your industry and website content as well as its PR value.

The days of obtaining all inbound links by whatever means are over now that Google has established the trend, which is nothing new, and the majority of the others have followed closely behind.

Low-quality and/or irrelevant inbound links won't only be of no benefit; they will actually result in a penalty.

In the long run, link farms, free-for-all link schemes, automatic link accumulation software, and other fads that don't thoroughly vet the links and the websites they originate from will cause more harm than good.

12. There's more to it than simply numbers and statistics. One of the closest business ties is probably the one between an internet business and SEO.

A SEO needs to understand the goals and desires of the business's founders in addition to the venture's statistics and data in order to be effective.

When looking for the "right fit" into the complicated world of the Internet, information that isn't often disclosed in a prospectus is frequently invaluable.

Due to my frequent calls and emails in the beginning, my own clients occasionally inquire, "Am I your only client?," to which I typically laugh and reply, "Yes, you are the only one that counts until I know your business almost as well as you do."

## Link-Building to Boost Page Rank and Traffic

Why do most websites have a links page? A site developer should take a links page into consideration for two key reasons.

1. One approach to make the search engines notice you is through search engine optimization, or SEO. Getting links is another important factor to remember if you want people to notice your website.

2. Your website provides links to other sites of interest that visitors may wish to visit, which is a service you are providing to them. Even though the retail sector may claim that they prefer visitors to stay on their website rather than visit any other sites, correctly selected links may be able to increase visitors' interest in the item you are selling! You might need to use creative thinking!

There appear to be both good and terrible links in the view of a search engine. Good links will boost your page rankings and place you at the top of the listings, while bad links will, at best, be ignored and, at worst, may work against you by causing your site to be ranked far lower.

A good link is one that comes from a website that is very relevant to yours and has a high page rank.

A bad link is one that clearly comes from a link farm and has no relevant links to your websites.

Before moving on, let's briefly discuss page rank. The rating that Google assigns to website pages, known as page rank, demonstrates their significance in Google's eyes.

The Google Toolbar, which is available for free download at http://toolbar.google.com, is a helpful tool because it can show you the page rank of any website you are visiting.

A website's page rank (or PR) runs from 0 to 10; 0 is the starting point, and 10 would be extraordinary!

The movement through the numbers is probably on a logarithmic scale, meaning that a site ranking 2 is several times more important than that ranked 1, not only by 1 point, even though Google maintains the techniques for calculating PR very secret.

You should strive to gain links to your site from websites with a higher page rank than your own while you are link building.

The search engines will be alerted right away by links from high-PR websites that your website is one they should index. The better, the more links!

Do you have to exclusively link to sites with better PageRank then?

The chances of you gaining any links for your brand-new website would be nil if everyone followed this advice!

Even while a site may currently have a ranking of 0, it might be actively attempting to improve, and you might gain from that effort.

Additionally, keep in mind that even if a site is not intended to help you with your rankings, human visitors may still find it valuable! Consequently, keep in mind these fundamental directives:

- Seek links from pages with high rankings.

- Add links to your page from any website that is highly relevant to yours.

First, consider the websites that visitors to your site might find beneficial to be able to access from there.

If you have a specialized website, for instance, are there any national organizations that support your sport, hobby, or line of work? Sending emails to these organizations to request reciprocal links with them should be your initial action.

This may resemble a David and Goliath battle, and many individuals are turned off by their new, amateurish website because they believe it to be far too small.

Your letters can go unanswered or you might get a rejection, but you never know! A major organization with a high page ranking might agree to link to you! Be ecstatic about this!

Put someone's link on your website as soon as they agree to a reciprocal connection with you, just in case they decide to check!

Now, consider your clients or visitors once more. Even though the big companies have declined to connect to you on their site, it might still be beneficial to include them on yours for the information of your visitors.

Never forget that getting website traffic is all about attracting and keeping repeat clients or visitors, not just search engine bots!

The challenging work has begun. Look for websites on the same topic as yours online that are definitely NOT competitors.

Search for websites with a higher page rank than your own while keeping an eye on the Google Toolbar; ideally, these sites should be in the top 4 or 5 positions (higher-ranked websites may be a touch condescending toward newer websites).

Can those who provide you with goods and services connect to your site? What about the public? Try to think creatively here; for example, if you run a sports website, why not include a link to a nearby photographer?

You can occasionally conduct effective research without a computer (yes, you can turn it off occasionally!).

Trade magazines are frequently an excellent place to start; send emails to any addresses listed and request a reciprocal link. Even if they currently do not have a links page, they might decide to add one in the future. Asking never hurts!

Verify that a links page exists when browsing websites. If they do, you might discover a form on which you can enter the information about your website and request that it be added to their links page or a button that makes it easy to recommend a new link for your website.

If a website doesn't seem to be canvassing links, you might need to email them. If there isn't a pertinent category for them to include your site in, don't be too discouraged; they can always add additional categories.

You won't receive what you don't ask for! If you do ask, you might get what you want!

Therefore, don't worry if someone emails you asking for a link exchange; just make sure you follow through on your commitment to post the links.

This may cause you to reevaluate your website since some visitors prefer not to have their link at the end of a lengthy page. To display more links, you should think using rotating banners, but keep the website straightforward. You may also need to block links that are not pertinent.

Show off your knowledge on the subject! The best way is to sign up for a forum, by the way.

Always include your website address in your signature when posting or responding to a topic on the forum. If forum users enjoy what they read about you, they will click on the link to visit your website, and voila!

You now have additional links coming into your site. If the user forum for your hosting provider provides a place where you may promote your new website, you might gain a lot of visitors from it. Beautiful links that are good for link spiders and search engines alike!

You can also leave your website address in the Guestbook of a relevant website. BUT ONLY IF IT IS A PERTINENT SITE, PLEASE!

Many people are unaware of or are unfamiliar with article writing as a tactic for generating links and traffic.

You probably have knowledge to impart to others or at the very least are an authority in your field. Create an article, then! Uncertain if you can? Start with the content of your website as a foundation instead because you might already have done the hard work. Lacking a topic to write about? Okay, let's do that again. What about a piece on the history of candle manufacture, for instance, if you sell creative candles?

There is surely something you can write about if you ponder long and hard enough! While some research may be necessary, articles will significantly increase your traffic and rating. (You can also use these as content on your own website, of course!)

The length of an article is not necessary; in fact, the shorter, and the better. No more than 600 to 1000 words, most likely.

Write about something relevant to your website in your content, that's what you want to do.

There are now a lot of websites where you can have your article published. Other websites are free to use your article, but they are required to credit you and link back to your website.

People who use your article will create links pointing back to it, and the more diverse the sites that use it, the better the links will be!

You can post your content to a variety of article sites, which is much better. One of the biggest is Ezine Articles, but there are many others that can be found by conducting a Google search.

No one can now claim that this is a simple task; it does require time. If your content is not well-written and offers readers something new, nobody will use it. It can't be monotonous either.

However, article posting is a really good strategy to boost the search engine ranking of your website and should not be disregarded.

Naturally, articles are valuable resources for Webmasters in another aspect as well—they provide free material for your website!

There are websites out there that cover a staggering array of topics and are both helpful and educational in and of themselves. You can find further hints and tips for optimizing your website, for instance, by reading free articles on web design.

You must provide the complete author bio and a link back to the original author's website if you utilize an article. However, the advantage for you is ready-made content that, ideally, is keyword-rich and will draw search engine bots to it like bees to honey.

Web rings are an additional method of creating links; once more, be sure the web ring you are joining has a high page rank. Web rings give you links and also list other interesting websites for your human visitors to browse.

Let's face it: creating and publishing a website is actually a lot more work than you probably initially anticipated while creating your home page.

But nothing is more discouraging than creating a beautiful website about which you are really proud, only to discover that it is completely empty.

You probably want to spend all of your time creating new pages and improving the ones you already have. Anything that takes you away from this will make you angry, but link building is necessary if you want your website to be successful.

The greatest idea is to set aside one day every week for your marketing operations. SEO and link development are incredibly time-consuming operations.

Create your pages with SEO in mind from the outset (or, to put it another way, think about the influence on spiders and bots as well as the human eye while you create your page!). Utilize your day once a week to create links.

The search engines will once again be suspicious if you try to obtain hundreds of links quickly, advise experienced experts in this field. Rather, just try to obtain one good connection at least once per month.

Website marketing is more like a marathon than a quick sprint. Numerous people will enter the race, but many will drop out. But if you accept that it will be difficult work and persevere, you will succeed.

There will come a time when you get a request for a reciprocal connection from a reliable, highly ranked website! Even while it might not be the end, you can be sure that it will make you feel great and that the majority of your efforts will have been worthwhile.

## Self-Employed SEO for Novices

You might want to handle your own website's SEO needs but have no idea where to begin. Most likely, you've wanted to get more involved with SEO for a long time but have never had the time.

Unfortunately, this is frequently brought on by the false belief that SEO is simple to use and does not require a lot of expertise. There are various ways to start doing SEO on your own and succeed, even though it does take time and experience.

Option 1: Develop your SEO expertise
The approach that will provide you the most personal delight while implementing SEO on your website is this one. Spend a lot of time reading online articles and books to get up to speed on the most recent SEO practices, trends, and strategies.

Then you want to start trying with various techniques you learn about, evaluate the outcomes, and update your website once again. This requires a significant investment of time, effort, patience, and resources and is part of the ongoing process of search engine optimization.

However, when you begin to reap the rewards of your labor after a few months, you will feel a tremendous lot of happiness.

This choice is advised if you wish to begin providing SEO services as a part of your business or if you are managing many websites.

This approach is probably not appropriate if you only have one website and do not want to offer SEO services to other businesses, given the amount of work needed to be successful.

Option 2: Look for a seasoned SEO manual
Most people who want to begin internet marketing on their own, learn more about the field, and not devote a lot of time to the endeavor should choose this choice.

Many SEO experts would be pleased to help you along the route and aid you in developing a fruitful web campaign. With this choice, a skilled professional will work with you to help you create a great campaign, so you won't have to learn everything on your own.

Your consultant might take care of the trickier parts of SEO while you took care of execution.

Your consultant could, for instance, help you create a list of keyword phrases, sample strategies for locating link partners, and usage instructions for title, alt, heading, bold, internal links, and meta tags.

You could ask the consultant to examine your work and make additional comments after you have done working on a few important pages. At first, you'll undoubtedly rely heavily on your consultant's guidance, but as you gain experience with SEO strategies and tactics, your reliance on your consultant will gradually decrease.

Progress reports delivered on a weekly or monthly basis are another crucial service your consultant ought to offer. They'll probably have access to programs that will let them produce reports on things like rankings, keyword phrases, incoming links, and other things.

The majority of the time, consultants can offer further helpful advice to aid in your company's online success on topics like PPC, conversion, usability, professional image, email campaigns, banner advertising, and other online marketing strategies.

Although this approach will take some investment from you, it is significantly less expensive than a full-service SEO package, and the cost will gradually go down as you develop your SEO skills.

How to Choose the Best Option

The most pertinent issue to ask yourself while choosing between these two methods is how much time you have to devote to SEO. Having an SEO consultant by your side will, in my opinion based on experience, cut down the amount of time you need to dedicate to your SEO project by roughly 50–75%. You must ascertain the level of industry competition.

The time needed to succeed might vary greatly depending on whether a business is a local pest treatment business or a large web hosting company. You will succeed no matter what route you take as long as you are committed and motivated!

## **SEO Moral**

The technique of optimizing a website with the aim of improving its positions in the Google search engine is known as ethical SEO, or search engine optimization if you prefer.

Depending on the website in issue and the keyphrases being sought, the real SEO process might be fairly involved.

The several methods could consist of, but not be limited to, optimizing alt tags, keyword density, and meta tags and header tags. Off-page optimization is also taken into account in addition to this.

Securing, retaining, and expanding relevant backlinks with certain anchor text configurations are all part of off page SEO tactics. This can significantly improve the rankings of particular keyphrases.

Because building backlinks has a beneficial impact on search engine results, some website owners have started to actively purchase backlinks in an effort to improve their rankings.

Google has been known to view this method as algorithm tampering, and it may have been worried that this may cause its search engine to produce less relevant results.

Due to this, Google is attempting to penalize those who purchase backlinks.

Although some believe that Google has overstepped its bounds in trying to punish webmasters for doing this, there is another perspective;

Building backlinks boosts a website's rankings since each backlink is viewed as a "vote," which is why Google does not want anyone buying links to boost their websites' rankings. People are effectively buying votes if they are purchasing backlinks! ... In the majority of social groups, this is frowned upon!

Off Page SEO efforts are still workable, though. The only thing that has changed is the approach. It is important to use techniques Google approves of rather than attempting to mislead it. This means that you should have high-quality material on your website (yeah, so technically this is On Page SEO, but it DOES make Off Page SEO easier!) High-quality content encourages links to your website from other sites.

The next step is to spread the word that your website has this excellent information. Some link-building strategies can be utilized for this, but not in an effort to trick Google; rather, use them to simply spread the word about your website.

Others will then wish to link to the useful information they discover!

There are several effective ways to achieve this, including articles, press releases, guest blog posts, and RSS feeds. We at kingpin-seo.co.uk consider this form of specialized off page SEO to be ethical SEO because it isn't meant to artificially influence Google results at all; rather, we offer Google exactly what it needs.

Backlinks should naturally develop if a website has tons of interesting, relevant content and information about it in prominent places online, which will encourage others to talk about it.

A fundamental but comprehensive way to view ethical SEO is that, for best results, ON PAGE and OFF PAGE SEO tactics must be applied methodically and in tandem.

### How to Quickly Index a Website

Get Indexed Quickly

What does a listing mean?

Every web page in the index is cached by the search engines.

This means in English that search engines copy and store information about every website they visit. That's what I mean, I think.

When you use a search engine, the returned pages typically contain ten results per page that are pertinent to your search.

In addition to a live "link" to the website, each result also contains a "cache" or "snap-shot" of the page that was taken the last time the spider visited it, sometime in the past.

A website must initially exist in order for it to be indexed. preferably one that you actually own, not one that is offered "free" like Geocities, etc.

A domain name registration only costs approximately $8, and cheap hosting only costs about $5 per month, but $10 per month will buy you very high-quality hosting.

I advise you to build a blog on your website in order to get ranked quickly. This can be done with any blog platform, but WordPress is the best in my opinion.

If you purchase high-quality hosting, cPanel and Fantastico scripts will be included. About 50 scripts in Fantastico Scripts are available for one-click automatic installation on your server. Among them is WordPress. You can also manually install WordPress if you choose.

It's time to get indexed in the search engines once you've developed the most basic, bare-bones website possible (Main page, half a dozen content pages, and a sitemap tying them all together).

If you like, you can "submit" your website to the search engines, but that is extremely time-consuming.

Here's where your blog comes into play: write content to it every day, without fail for the first three weeks at least, and make sure it's fascinating and pertinent to your website.

Set up your blog such that each time you publish a new post, it will automatically "ping" the blog directories.

Search engines absolutely adore blogs because they are dynamic — updated on a regular basis by their owners — as opposed to normal website pages which, for the most part, remain static — unchanged for months on end.

Here's what happens: Google, Yahoo, MSN and the other search engines are always looking for fresh content to serve up to their search visitors or clients, and one place they look for fresh content is in blogs.

The search engines will notice if you update your blog every day with new articles or other content, and they will start routinely visiting your site.

By providing a link to either my homepage or sitemap in the sidebar (menu) of my blog, I include a connection to my regular website pages.

After new content, "links" are the second-best thing that search engines adore... They actually live and die by links, so if they come across one someplace that they haven't seen before, they record it and follow it to wherever it may go. And if the link they discover is on your blog, you had better make sure it points to your website's sitemap. After you make it, click on it to confirm that it does.

As soon as users visit your website, Yahoo and MSN will list the pages and typically index them within a few days. People can find them in search results as soon as they are indexed.

And that's how simple it is to rank highly.

## Link Building's Importance for SEO

Making search engines aware of the significance of your website is the simplest approach to raise its ranking. How do you go about that?

Well, link building is the most effective method. The act of getting other websites to link to your own involves link building. Your website's "link popularity" will rise if other websites link to it, and because search engines will view your website as essential, you should see an increase in visitors.

The reason why most websites rank so poorly in the search engines is because link development takes a lot of work. Unbeknownst to many website owners, link popularity can have a significant impact on how well a website ranks in search engines. For you, this is good news. Establish your "web cred" by beginning to build links.

## Page Rank's importance

Google, the most widely used search engine on the Internet, uses Page Rank to gauge how popular a website's links are. All you need to do is download the Google Toolbar to see a website's Page Rank. Every website you visit will have its Page Rank shown in the toolbar as a tiny green bar. The Page Rank of a website might range from zero to ten.

If your website has a low or no Page Rank, don't worry. While many websites only have a Page Rank of 1 or 2, the most well-known websites on the Internet have a Page Rank of 8 or 9.

## Quality Matters

Search engines examine for more than just the quantity of links pointing to a website. Getting quality links is the process's most crucial step. Links with a high Page Rank are considered to be quality links. The ideal link comes from a website with a high Page Rank, though any site with a Page Rank of 1 or above is helpful. Search engines also take into account the subject matter of a website that links to you.

It is best to obtain links from websites related to the sector of business in which you are engaged. For instance, since website design is my line of work, I try to get the majority of my links from websites that are also relevant to web design.

## Acquiring Links

Offering high-quality and educational information to your readers and hoping for natural links is one of the finest ways to increase your link popularity. They will inevitably connect to your website from theirs if they find the content compelling enough.

The quickest and simplest technique to get some inbound links is definitely through directory submissions. However, the value that Internet directories can offer to your Page Rank is diminished by all the other links because they link to thousands of other websites. The Open Project Directory (http://www.dmoz.org) is the only directory that requires submissions. It is then best to look through local or more specialized directories. Search engines will learn which region(s) you serve if you submit your website to Canadian, Ontario, and even Windsor web directories. Then, to let search engines know about your line of business, you should submit to directories linked to your industry. You may locate these types of directories via a Google search.

Writing articles is a wonderful way to increase inbound connections to your website if you consider yourself to be a talented writer. These articles can then be sent to websites for article syndication, where other website owners are free to utilize your material on their own. However, there is a catch: in exchange for using the piece, they must provide a link back to your website. If you join in a discussion forum for your industry but lack the motivation or time to produce an article, you're in luck. Just keep in mind to sign off with a link to your website.

Reciprocal linking is the final strategy for generating high-quality inbound connections. This kind of tactic entails getting in touch with other webmasters and suggesting a link exchange. Simply send an email to a few relevant, non-competitive websites to see if they're interested. It's preferable if their link is already on a page of your website before the offer.

It's Vital to Use Linking Text

It is essential that you try to include targeted key words in your link whenever you use one of the aforementioned linking strategies. This material is examined by search engines to understand the purpose of your website. Try to include "Red Widgets" in your link text if your website contains them.

In Conclusion

When aiming to rank well in the search engines, link popularity is crucial. The significance of link analysis to search engines will only increase, not decrease.

This method of measuring a website's relevance is legitimate and impervious to manipulation. Because link building takes time, it must be given top attention in your Internet marketing campaigns. The earlier you start, the better.

www.ingramcontent.com/pod-product-compliance
Lightning Source LLC
Chambersburg PA
CBHW070857260726
48661CB00004B/1459